Look Up! Salisbury

GW00602054

By Christopher Newberry and Rodney Graham

A tour of Salisbury's historic city centre above the eye-line, with stories from behind its façades

why **look up?**

The high streets of British cities and towns have developed over the centuries as places of trade and commerce, with the street-level shopfront presenting the focus of attention to prospective customers. Most of the buildings in Salisbury's commercial area were built between the reign of two Edwards: Edward I, 'Longshanks', and Edward VII son of Victoria. What the buildings had in common was that they were designed as a single composition: the shop front, which we describe as the 'commercial waterline', and the premises above working in architectural harmony. Often these buildings were erected by individuals who wanted to stamp their 'mark' on the city. They invested a lot of money in fine architectural detail, which showed-off wealth and confidence in their business. It was an investment which made them the talk of the town!

Sadly, most of the original shopfronts have disappeared. Most have been replaced by unsympathetic storefronts with enormous shop windows meant to attract us to their goods and services – not the architecture. That means we are missing out on the original design and history of the buildings. So, we are inviting you to look above this 'commercial waterline', above the shopfront. Turn the page to see what we mean . . .

▲ *This butchers' on Fish Row, is one of very few shops where its front is still an integral part of its character.*

◀ *47 Fisherton Street, at a time when the shop front was an integral part of the building.*

imagine . . .

that Salisbury's High Street is submerged in water up to the 'commercial waterline'. All the shopfronts are under water. All we can see are the buildings above the ground floor. The view and perception of this historic city completely changes! Even if you've lived in Salisbury all your life, in this book you will discover features of the city centre you may never have noticed.

Salisbury has been around for a long time. Since Neolithic times there was a settlement on the nearby hilltop of Old Sarum. Then in the Iron Age, it became a fort, which the Romans called "Sorviodunum". The Saxons called it 'Searesbyrig'. When the Normans arrived, they moved the town to its present site and called it 'Saresberie' and then 'Sarum'. Why 'Sarum'? Well, in those days documents were written in Latin and the way they abbreviated 'Saresberie,' was by writing 'Sar' with a stroke over the 'r', which was a common symbol for the Latin ending 'um'.

We have selected some of the outstanding buildings in Salisbury's city centre and look at each one as it might have appeared in the mind of its architect or designer: clean, horizontal and perpendicular lines; no perspective and no background to distract. The essence of the building.

We take you on a 'tour' of Salisbury's city centre starting at Fish Row, just off the Market and ending at the North Gate, leading to the Close. This tour will reveal a fascinating view of the buildings, bringing up close a lot of the details we usually strain to find – and some of the landmarks that make this historic city what it is.

With the help of this guide book you will discover parts of the Salisbury of old. On the next page you will find a map to guide you, starting, if you like, at the Tourist Information Centre (or jump around, if you prefer). Just **be careful when you cross the streets!** Make sure you look left and right before you …

look up !

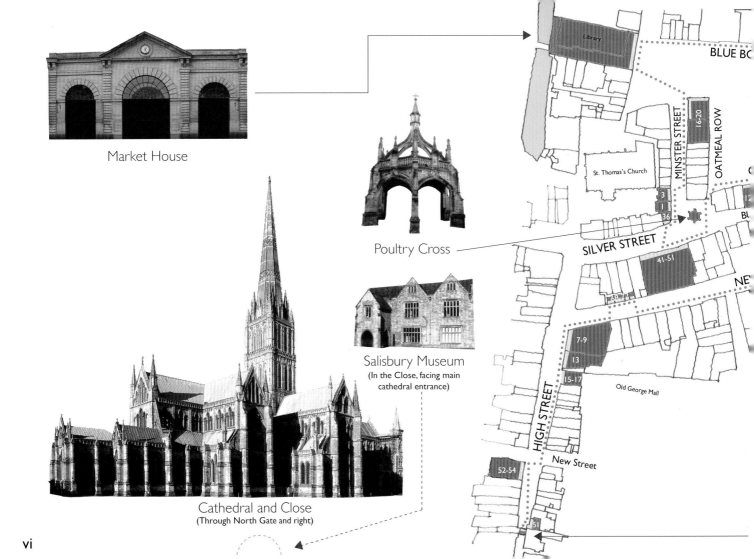

Market House

Poultry Cross

Salisbury Museum
(In the Close, facing main
cathedral entrance)

Cathedral and Close
(Through North Gate and right)

Library

BLUE BO

MINSTER STREET

OATMEAL ROW

16-20

St. Thomas's Church

3
1
36

BL

SILVER STREET

41-51

NE

7-9

13

15-17

Old George Mall

HIGH STREET

New Street

52-54

51

The Look Up! Route

WINCHESTER STREET

QUEEN STREET

BROWN STREET

FISH ROW

MILFORD STREET

47
51
3-5
13-15
8
8
15
6

War Memorial

Guildhall and Tourist Information Centre

North Gate

	Building
	Front elevation
	Route

8 Queen Street

Built:	1425
Materials:	Timber framed
Original purpose:	Home
Key feature:	Leaded window panes

'The glaziers' work before substantial was
I must confess, thrice as much lead as glass,
Which in the suns' meridian cast a light,
As it had been within an hour of night'
- From the poem, "The wonders of the Peake"
by Charles Cotton (1630-1687)

This half-timbered building has a jettied façade, which in the fifteenth century meant that the owner was seriously wealthy. A jettied façade is an elevation pushed out on timber brackets at the upper floor levels. Windows were also a sign of wealth. Each window consists of a rectangular timber casement holding a diamond shaped pattern of pieces of glass held in place by lead glazing bars called 'cames'. Although probably no longer original, the windows reflect a pattern that existed in the 15th century. Later seventeenth century equivalents were similar in construction but had rectangular glass panes. The lead cames and glass pieces were stiffened with cast iron rods to which the glazed panel would be fixed with wire. These had the function of resisting the pressure of wind on the face of the glazed panel – without them, the panel would collapse. Although the windows are large, they let in little natural light because of the large proportion of lead came to glass.

Local legend has it that this house was owned by medieval merchant, John A'Port. Historians say otherwise – he lived near Market House – but why spoil a good story? It would appear that there were two John A'Ports; father and son. The first died in 1456 aged about 60. The second was born in 1420 and died in 1485. The father made his fortune mostly dealing in wool, though he seems to have had his finger in many-a-pie: in 1427 he was importing fruit, iron, soap, tiles and wine. He also imported fish, such as herring and salmon, from Ireland and Iceland. His son carried on in the same vein but, in addition to being wealthy, he played a big role in local and national politics. Again, like John Halle,

John A'Port actually owned a ship, based in Southampton, which he used to import products from France, Ireland and Iceland. This sort of ship is a 'cog', with its single square sail. Though slow, it could carry a lot of weight. ▶

John A'Port the younger was a very powerful man who could rival the Bishop of Salisbury – and often did. At the local level, he was mayor of Salisbury six times. On the national level in 1457, while the War of the Roses was raging, he was commissioned to do a very important job for King Henry V: he had to determine the number of archers that Wiltshire would be providing for the Lancastrian cause. However by 1471 John had switched sides. He helped Edward IV, of the House of York, recover Kent from the grasp of a supporter of the House of Lancaster, Thomas the Bastard (for thus was he known). The Bastard's army was defeated, but he escaped to Southampton where he was caught, imprisoned and beheaded. His head was set on a spike on London Bridge "looking into Kentward".

▲ *At the Battle of Agincourt in 1415, the longbowmen played a pivotal role in Henry V's victory.*

In John A'Port's time the English longbow played a pivotal role in warfare. The longbow was a difficult weapon to master, but used in large numbers it was very effective. The bow was about 2 metres long (6'6") and the arrows could pierce armour and chain mail. Longbowmen could shoot 10 arrows per minute. At Agincourt 7000 of the 9000 English soldiers were longbowmen, so the French had 70,000 arrows raining on them per minute. In comparison, each French crossbow could only shoot 3 per minute. What was the secret of the English success? Well, it was law that all men, including peasants and villeins, had to practise archery on pain of death. John A'Port's job was to ensure that the king could count on Wiltshire longbowmen.

◀ *14th century English longbowman.*

9

5 Ox Row (10 Butcher Row)

Built:	Early 18th century
Materials:	Timber frame, clay tiles
Original purpose:	Shop
Key feature:	Original bow windows, hung sashes

This building is distinguished by its three-bay, curve sided sliding sash windows, known as 'bow windows'. The proportions of the bow windows, which are provided at both first and second floors, are well suited to the narrowness of the building. It is thought to be of early to mid 18th century in origin. The top of the building is finished with a clay tiled gable, enclosing the attic, which is fronted by a balcony with elegant wrought iron railings.

Bow windows were commonly found in Georgian shop fronts and public houses and inns, because they naturally project their presence and importance into the streetscape. In fact, the London Building Act of 1774 restricted their projection to no more than ten inches to prevent them interfering with street activity. The bow window was always an expensive feature, notably because, unlike a flat segmented bay window, it required the joiner to make all the horizontal sections of timber in the frame and sash itself to be curved *(see box on page 9)*. Traditionally the glass too would have been curved, making it very expensive compared to the flat plate glass that was more readily available. It is therefore little surprise to see a decline in the use of bow windows between the 18th and 19th centuries and a trend to 'flatten' windows onto the elevation.

The top one is a bay window, with angled frames, whereas the bottom one is a bow window, with curved frames. ▶

◀ **Bow window.**

These are the 14th century precursors of 'fast food': Market ▲ *cooks. They had a terrible reputation because of their lack of hygiene and, frankly, rather foul-tasting food. Nevertheless, poor city dwellers without cooking facilities at home, had little choice but to rely on these market cooks for sustenance.*

People have been coming to Salisbury market on Tuesdays since 1227, when King Henry III granted the city's bishop, Richard Poore, a charter allowing a weekly market and a yearly fair. In those days the vast majority of people lived in the countryside and were usually self-sufficient for food, but Salisbury was an urban area. Most poor city dwellers lived in very cramped conditions, without a kitchen or even basic cooking equipment. A few might have had a kettle in which to make 'pottage' – a sort of stew made of vegetables, water and barley or oats. The wealthy could add meat. Lacking the means, poor people got much of their food from vendors or cooks. People could go to a cook shop with their own ingredients and a cook would prepare the meal in his kitchen or they could buy ready-made hot meals – a sort of 'fast food'. These vendors and cooks had a terrible reputation and certainly were not the most salubrious of caterers. No matter where the food came from, everyone, including children, washed it down with a great mug of ale – you just couldn't trust the water. How things have changed! Today the market has a great source of fast food: fish and chips. It is believed that the first 'fish and chips' were dished out by a Jewish immigrant called Joseph Malin in East London in about 1860. Soon fish & chips wrapped in newspaper was as Victorian as steam and smoke. For many years fish & chips was the favourite British 'fast food' (recently ousted by the burger and the pizza). However there is one habit that has remained from medieval times: fish and chips is still often washed down by ale … though now you have to be 18.

Credit photo: Brendan McGhee

11

6 - 7 Ox Row (12 Butcher Row)

Built:	Mid 18th century
Materials:	Brick
Original purpose:	Two homes
Key feature:	Top floor original windows with false heads

This three-storey building of mid 18th-century origin was constructed as two separate houses, later amalgamated into a single entity for use as shop. The elevation has been carefully composed to give the effect of a single building and the upper windows, which sit below the brick gable with timber pediment, have used the Palladian style of the Venetian window. Venetian windows became popular to builders who were keen to give their houses some individuality. In this case they offer the elevation a sense of robust presence and unity.

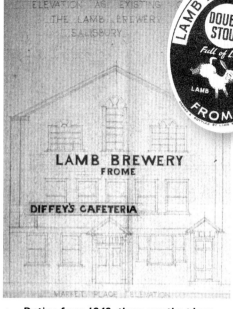

▲ Dating from 1949, these are the plans to change the signboards of Diffey's Cafeteria and Lamb Brewery.

At present Charter 1227 Restaurant (so named because of the charter granted to Salisbury in 1227 – see page 11) occupies this building, but for more than 100 years it was a coffee house and pub owned by the Lamb Brewery. Throughout the 19th and 20th centuries, Lamb was one of the most important breweries in England, rivalling the mighty Fullers. In fact, both Fullers and Lamb claim to have had their origins in the same Chiswick brewhouse. The Lamb was founded in 1853 by the brothers John and Thomas Bailey. At one point they owned more than 70 pubs, including this one. According to Kelly's Directory, in 1875 this building was occupied by the Lamb Brewery with Barnard William as the landlord. It remained a Lamb pub until at least the 1950's, when the brewery lost its identity through a series of take-overs culminating in becoming a part of Usher's. The Lamb Brewery was famous for its strong ales at a time when both working and middle class people preferred beer to wine. However, it must be said that the middle classes preferred the sparkling pale ales to the rather murky strong milds of the working classes.

How times change

In 1775 the landlord of the Half Moon Tavern at 6 - 7 Ox Row thanks his customers:

J. Ravenscroft takes this public method of returning his sincere thanks to those gentlemen who have been so kind as to favour him with their encouragement since he entered on the above tavern; and begs leave humbly to solicit the support and assistance of the gentlemen and tradesmen of this city and neighbourhood, in his present undertaking, assuring them that he will most earnestly endeavour, by an obliging behaviour, reasonable charges, and a strict attention to their commands, to merit their future favours.

- Salisbury & Winchester Journal, 4 December 1775.

In 2008 the landlords of Harpers Restaurant at 6 - 7 Ox Row thank their customers: *Harpers has been sold. Adrian & Annie would like to thank all customers for their support over the years. The restaurant has been bought by Danny Bozic, formerly of the Barford Inn. Under it's new name, Charter 1227 Restaurant, we wish him luck.*

- Harpers website, 14 November 2008

10 - 11 Ox Row (18 Butcher Row)

Built:	1594
Materials:	Timber and terracotta hanging tiles
Original purpose:	Inn
Key feature:	Bargeboard

This building, like most on Ox Row, has two faces: one on the Market side, the other on Butcher Row (see opposite page). The Butcher Row façade reveals the true age of the building – 1594 – while this side would have us believe it was a Victorian structure. It was then that the ground floor was bricked-in and the hanging tiles and bargeboard were added. A bargeboard or 'vergeboard' is a timber board which is fixed to the gable end of a roof. It disguises and protects the projecting rafter and exposed purlin ends. Bargeboard designs can be used to date a building. This one, for example looks typically mid-Victorian, carved with cusps along the lower edge. Later, Edwardian bargeboards tended to be rather more plain. They can be ornately decorated too. A fine example of a richly decorated bargeboard can be found at Ockwells in Berkshire, a timber framed 15th century manor house described by Nikolaus Pevsner as "the most refined and the most sophisticated timber framed mansion in England".

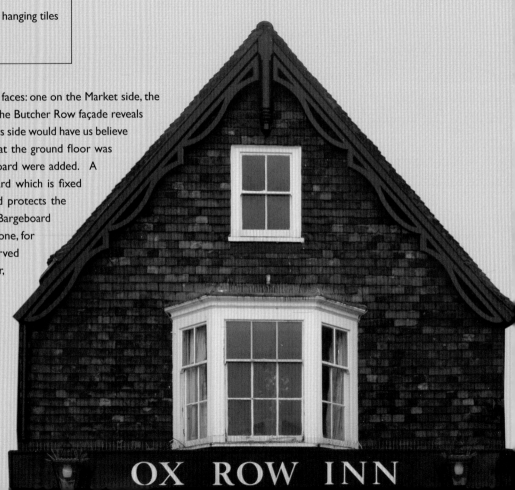

OX ROW INN

The medieval mind was a very ordered one. Feudal society was strictly divided into 'those who pray, those who fight and those who work'. There was no escape from class determined by birth. Everyone accepted this order. With that same mentality, the market was divided into strict areas of activity. Wool was sold at the Wool Cross, milk at the Milk Cross, poultry at the Poultry Cross. In 1227 Butcher Row, which now backs Ox Row, was where animals were bought and slaughtered on the spot. A messy affair. What to do with the blood, bones and entrails? For four hundred years, Salisbury's butchers maintained a foot bridge, called Pudding Bridge, from which they dumped the entrails into the river ('entrails' were known as 'pudding' in those days). At first Butcher Row was literally a row of stalls – no buildings. Over the years, little by little, the stalls became more durable, more permanent, until finally there was the row of buildings which now constitute Ox Row.

By the end of the 18th century, Salisbury's Beast Market was huge. According to the Salisbury and Winchester Journal of 24 August 1782, "Our Fortnight's Market for Fat Cattle is become the largest in England, Smithfield excepted. There were upwards of 400 beasts, and 2000 sheep and lambs, in the market on Tuesday last; very few remained unsold. The cattle fetched a very good price". At that time, the Ox Row Inn was called the City Arms and was the venue for the annual Feast of Graziers and Butchers. Most guests were both graziers and butchers; they owned and fed the animals – and slaughtered them. The Salisbury and Winchester Journal advertised the event: "Notice is hereby given,

Scene from an 18th century cattle market by Jan Josef Horemans the Elder. ▲

that the Annual Feast for the Graziers and Butchers will be held at John Webb's, at the City Arms, on Monday the 19th of August; when it is hoped that all whom it may concern, will attend, to celebrate in a friendly manner so laudable an undertaking, as the continuance of the Great Market has proved to be. Dinner on table at two o'clock". Then a few days later the same journal reported: "The Annual Feast of the Graziers and Butchers was held at the City Arms, in the Market-place, on Monday last. There was a respectable appearance of company, and the day was spent in the greatest harmony and festivity". In other words, a good time was had by all …

This is the Butcher Row façade. The timber frame tells us that it was built in the 16th century, but the Ox Row side looks completely Victorian because the ground floor was bricked in and the hanging tiles and bargeboard were added then. ▶

12 Ox Row (24 Butcher Row)

Built:	1890's
Materials:	Brick and stone
Original purpose:	Shop
Key feature:	Faience

This building's façade is very intriguing. It's highly decorative, composed of numerous materials – basically brick and stone, but also glazed earthenware tiles called faience. The tiles were made specifically for Walter Hart, the shop's owner at the end of the 19th century. On the Dutch gable there is a shell motif made of Bath Stone, which is showing typical signs of decay. Just peering out of the shell, there is a young child's head. This is known as a 'putto', which is Latin for "little man". Although the putto has wings, it is similar to (but not the same as) a cherub. Unlike the cherub, the putto is a secular character, not a religious one. Its origins lie in the ancient Greco-Roman world. The putto was a sort of helper of the god of love – Eros in Greek mythology or Cupid in Roman. His role was to facilitate profane love between two people. The inclusion of a putto may have been a purposeful act on the part of the building's owner. Perhaps by including him, the owner might influence his own personal life?

FISH GAME HART POULTRY ICE

PATISSERIE VALERIE

Est 1926

▲ *Faience tiles with Art Nouveau influence made specially for Walter Hart's shop.*

This is an interesting and moving story, but complicated, so read carefully! Walter William Hart was a butcher by profession. He learned his trade just down the lane on Butcher Row with W.J. Snook. After completing his apprenticeship, Walter set up shop and lived at this address (see 'Hart' on the sign over what is now the patisserie). He married Priscilla and they had seven children, the last of which was born in 1895 when Walter was 43. It seems to have been a successful business because he had several employees – among them a young woman half his age named Alice. In 1896 she became pregnant and had a son she named William, later known as Bill. Walter was the father. Life must have been difficult for him – he died when he was only 52. According to the coroner's report that investigated his death, this is what happened: one day in 1903 Walter went to visit his sister at her home near Andover in Hampshire. He spent the day playing dominoes and shooting small birds, which he brought into the house to count how many he'd shot. He played with his nephews in the garden and went to the local pub where a witness said he had "never seen him more cheerful in his life". According to his sister it had been "a happy day". The next morning he was found dead on the garden steps, with the hunting gun lying next to him. The coroner's verdict was suicide. Priscilla, his wife had to carry on with the business to support her seven children, the youngest of which was only eight.

This was the delivery van used by Walter Hart at about the time of his death. Above is an account book (credit before credit cards) from 1907. Note that "P. Hart" – Priscilla – is ◀ running the business.

Bill, with wife, Dora, and first son, Hector. Dora died tragically aged only 25, leaving three children in the care of Bill. Eva, Dora's sister, had a child who died in the same year as Dora, his aunt. Bill later married Eva. ▶

Walter's illegitimate son, Bill, grew up, set up a business and married Dora Drewett. Tragically, she died aged only 25, leaving Bill with three children, the first of which was born in 1919. Dora had a sister named Eva, who had had a child out of wedlock. Tragedy struck again – the child died aged two in the same year that his aunt Dora had died. Bill later married Eva and together, they brought up the three children. Many of Bill and Dora's descendents still live in Salisbury today.

The Poultry Cross

Erected:	Late 15th century
Materials:	Portland stone
Original purpose:	Market cross
Key feature:	Flying buttresses

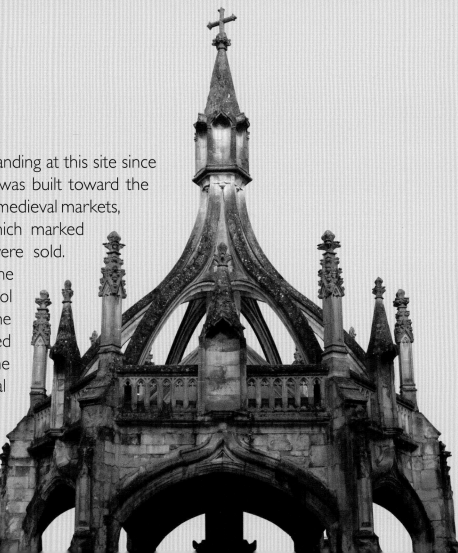

Although there has been a cross standing at this site since at least 1307, this particular cross was built toward the end of the 15th century. As in most medieval markets, Salisbury had a lot of crosses, which marked the area where certain goods were sold. There was the Livestock Cross, the Cheese & Milk Cross and the Wool and Yarn Cross. Poultry Cross is the last one remaining. It was restored in 1711 and again in 1852, when the flying buttresses rising to the central pinnacle were added by Owen Browne-Carter, a Winchester-based architect. By the way, the buttresses are purely ornamental, they don't support anything.

Owen Browne-Carter had two principal connections with Salisbury. The first was his restoration of the Poultry Cross in 1852. The second was his death in 1859.

He was born in London in 1806 and trained for ten years with William Garbett, Architect to the Dean and Chapter of Winchester Cathedral. He was a brilliant illustrator: he travelled for two years recording temples and buildings in Egypt along the Nile and in Cairo. His illustrations form the basis of *Illustrations of Cairo*, the only book ever published by Robert Hay, one of the earliest 'egyptologists'. As an architect he is best known for the Corn Exchange in Winchester (now the main library); his neo-gothic churches – particularly St. Matthews in Otterbourne – and his restorations, such as The Great Hall in Winchester and, of course, the Poultry Cross.

◀ *An 1810 engraving depicting the Poultry Cross before its restoration in 1852. Notice that the flying buttresses surrounding the central pinnacle have not yet been built.*

While in his early twenties, Owen Browne-Carter was employed as an illustrator to travel through Egypt for two years. His employer was Robert Hay, a young, wealthy Scotsman and one of the first 'egyptologists'. This is one of Browne-Carter's illustrations, which appeared in Hay's only published book, Illustrations of Cairo. ▶

Browne-Carter was also responsible for training one of the most important architects of Victorian times, George Edmund Street, who designed the Royal Courts of Justice on the Strand,

Despite all his ability and his success, soon after restoring the Poultry Cross, Owen Browne-Carter died, age 53, in Bugmore Hospital – Salisbury's pest house – alone and a pauper.

One of Owen Browne-Carter's best known works is his design of Winchester's Corn Exchange, now the Discovery Centre, which includes the public library. ▶

41 - 51 Silver Street

Built:	1890
Materials:	Applied timber and render
Original purpose:	Pharmacy and offices
Key feature:	Tudor Revival style

The late nineteenth century saw the beginnings of the Tudor Revival style, largely as a reaction to the Victorian Gothic Revival style. Tudor Revival took many different forms, one of which was what is known as 'Mock Tudor'. Mock Tudor echoed the picturesque half-timbered cottage of Tudor times. The infill of stucco render gave it that well-known 'black and white' appearance. The telltale difference between Tudor and Mock Tudor is the straightness and regularity of the timber sections. In the case of Mock Tudor the visible timbers are not an integral part of the structure: they are applied to the surface. In contrast, the original Tudor timbers form the structural frame of the building. The timbers were hewn with an axe directly from tree trunks and boughs, chosen specifically for their length and shape and connected using precisely cut dry joints and timber pegs. Boots The Chemist, built many of its stores using such 'half-timbered-looking' buildings, which appear in many towns and cities across the country. An interesting aspect of this building is its reverse elevation on New Canal, which is very different and clearly of a later period – possibly 1930's. It has a whiff of Arts and Crafts, suggested by the composition of its bands of windows: a row of small ones offset by much larger ones below and topped by square roof dormers above (see right).

pharmacy   *Boots*   beauty

The story of Neal McNamee and Eileen O'Leary is a story of people trying hard to better themselves, only to have their dreams destroyed by fate. Neal was born a catholic in Ireland in 1884. His father William was a poor man who couldn't read or write himself, but made sure all five of his children got an education. Neal was clever and hard working – by the time he was 27 years old he had worked his way up to being a Provisions Manager for Lipton Grocers. Eileen was of Irish descent, but protestant. Born in 1892, she attended St. Thomas's school in Salisbury. Neal and Eileen met when they both worked at the Lipton store at 41 Silver Street (next to Starbucks). Lipton stores were then what Sainsbury's is to our time. Sir Thomas Lipton was the founder not only of the stores, but of the well-known Lipton tea.

Neal's good work had been personally followed by Sir Thomas, who offered him a job in Philadelphia, USA. For Neal this was a great opportunity and he accepted. Neal and Eileen were married in January 1912, when he was 27 and she 19. They were both obviously very well regarded in the Salisbury community. He had received a personal letter of introduction from Sir Thomas, while she got a letter of recommendation from the baptist church pastor and then mayor of Salisbury, William Prichard. He also gave her a traveller's bible as a

Lipton Grocers at 41 Silver Street in about 1911. The man in the centre could be Neal and the third person from the right looks like Eileen. ▶

◀ *Reverse side, seen from New Canal.*

◀ ***Neal and Eileen McNamee met while working at Lipton Grocers.***

going away present. Their trip to America would be a honeymoon and a passage to a new life. Knowing they would be sailing, she purchased a blouse with a little anchor embroidered at the front. Neal and Eileen boarded the Titanic on the 10th of April 1912. They were third class passengers. Neither survived. Even in death there was class inequality. The bodies of first class passengers were brought back home. Eileen's body was buried at sea. She was wearing the embroidered blouse and had her wedding ring on her finger – she had the bible in her purse. His body was never found.

Peter Daniels Archive

36 Silver Street

Built:	1428
Materials:	Timber frame
Original purpose:	House
Key feature:	'Picket fence' window pattern

Unlike the building featured on page 20, this is an authentic half-timbered Tudor building, bequeathed to Trinity Hospital by John Wynchestre in 1458. As with many buildings of this period, there have been extensive alterations and internal refitting. The timbers in buildings of this period are often crooked and jagged, but this structure's frame is built from quite straight timbers (with the exception the curved wind-braces to the roof). The straight timbers suggest that this building was constructed at a time when there was plenty of timber available, whereas at other times, during periods of considerable deforestation, builders had less choice regarding shape. As with all timber framed buildings of this period the timber sections were selected directly from trees by the highly skilled carpenters of the day. Once felled, the section of timber required would be cut by hand and the surfaces of the timbers smoothed with a tool called an adze, similar to an axe, but with the blade positioned horizontally, rather than vertically. After cutting to size, the timbers forming the posts, beams and braces would have their ends prepared for jointing using similar mortice and tenon cuts that can be found in furniture making. These joints would be connected using wooden pegs.

It would appear that the first occupant of this house, built in 1428, was a man by the name of John Wynchestre, a barber. In those days barbers were also dentists and surgeons. They did everything from cutting hair, to pulling teeth, to administering enemas, to amputating limbs. John wouldn't have had to attend medical school to become a surgeon – it was a trade, like being a baker, a cobbler ... or a butcher. In fact, it wasn't until after John's death that surgery was studied at university level. However, he may have been a member of the 'Company of Barbers'. Between battles against the Lancastrians in the War of the Roses, Edward IV somehow found time to set up the Company of Barbers.

John spoke 'Middle English', a language similar to Chaucer's, and he would have had very limited access to books, as Gutenberg hadn't yet got 'round to inventing the printing press. John would have obtained his knowledge from word of mouth or perhaps from a hand-written book such as *Mirror of Phlebotomy and Practice of Surgery* by John of Arderne. To do his job, John needed knowledge about anatomy, medicine and, very importantly, astrology. In the medieval mind, health was controlled by humours in the body and these were controlled by the position of astral bodies. For example, the arms and hands were ruled by Gemini, the head and face by Aries, the chest by Cancer, and so on. According to this theory, remedies were least effective when the parts of the body were under the influence of their star sign. So, for example, treating an in-grown toe nail would be most difficult between 20 February and 20 March because that's when Pisces, ruler of the feet, was strongest. We don't know how successful John Wynchestre was as a

An English barber, from about the time of ▲ John Wynchestre, engaged in one of his many jobs: extracting a tooth. The plaque above is found at this house and reads: "This house built in 1428 was bequeathed to the hospital of the Holy Trinity by John Wynchestre (Barber) A.D.1447 . . . "

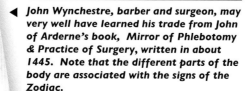

◄ *John Wynchestre, barber and surgeon, may very well have learned his trade from John of Arderne's book, Mirror of Phlebotomy & Practice of Surgery, written in about 1445. Note that the different parts of the body are associated with the signs of the Zodiac.*

surgeon. By today's standards, probably not very successful at all, but as a barber he must have been very busy because during his lifetime clean shaven faces were in fashion – indeed in some areas beards were prohibited by the church! Upon his death in 1458, John Wynchestre left his house to the Trinity Hospital on condition that "the Master and Brothers of the Hospital should hold his obit for his soul and for the soul of Agnes his wife on Friday in the first week of Lent in the Church of St. Thomas the Martyr".

1 Minster Street

Built:	Mid-15th century
Materials:	Timber and render
Original purpose:	Hostelry
Key feature:	Jettied floor

HAUNCH OF VENISON

As charming in appearance as the Haunch of Venison may seem, it is a superb example of just how such a building has been significantly altered since it was first constructed – to the point that it becomes a hotchpotch of architectural styles. Its elevation to Minster Street displays an array of building features, from its 14th century origins, up to the Victorian period when it was probably last re-configured.

The building is composed of a rendered timber framed elevation (exposed timber posts are still visible to the corners of the first floor). The 2nd floor is jettied as it would have been since its origins, but this feature has been rendered in and a lead drip added. The windows on the second floor are casements, but clearly of a much later period. The first floor elevation has had two sliding sash windows with plain glass incorporated, probably in Georgian or Victorian times. These are very large features in comparison to the size of the original windows. The hand-painted signs are a significant visual feature of the building, but may well be relatively recent additions.

However, as with any listed building such as this, all of the features of the building – however different from the original – become protected, thus ensuring the longevity of all the features from the many architectural periods represented.

Old buildings are full of stories. The further back in time one goes, the more unreliable the story. The Haunch of Venison is one such old building: 'it is said' that in 1320 the establishment was used as accommodation for workmen building the cathedral, but by then the cathedral had been completed for 50 years – except for the spire and tower. Maybe that's what they were building. 'They say' that in the 14th century it was a brothel for the clergy. 'It is said' that to avoid embarrassment, a tunnel was built to connect it to the Church of St. Thomas. 'They say' that the oak beams supporting the building were

◀ *Unsurprisingly, neither of the Haunch of Venison's ghosts has ever been photographed – this is a late 19th century try-on.*

taken from disused sailing vessels. This is disputed by experts who reckon it would have been too expensive and too ill-fitting. 'It is said' that the Haunch of Venison is haunted by ghosts. For centuries people have complained of feeling weirdly cold in certain rooms and of having things go missing only to reappear somewhere else. One of these ghosts is the Grey Lady, forever searching for her lost child. The other ghost is the Demented Whist Player who, when caught cheating, had his hand chopped off by a butcher and thrown into a disused oven. For years the hand lay in the ashes until it was found in the 19th century during refurbishment. What we cannot doubt is that there actually is a severed, mummified hand, there for all to see – except the ghost who, 'it is said', continues to wander through the building looking for his hand. This story does not end there. In 2010 the mummified hand was stolen from its showcase, but it has since been returned (see *The Independent* article right).

It is said that a building established here in about 1320 was used as accommodation for workers building the cathedral spire. ▲

THE INDEPENDENT

Mummified hand stolen from Haunch of Venison pub

Tuesday, 16 March 2010

Thieves took an unusual trophy from a Wiltshire pub – a mummified hand amputated from a cheating gambler.

The macabre relic was held in a locked glass case at the Haunch of Venison in Salisbury. It is believed to have been cut off a gambler caught cheating during a game of whist. It clutches a pack of 18th-century playing cards and is rumoured to be cursed.

Thieves came prepared last week as they unscrewed the cabinet to take the hand, which was originally found during renovation work.

Chantelle Stefan, barmaid at the 684-year-old pub. "It's a mummified hand of a card player that cheated," she said. "The butcher chopped his hand off years ago and threw it into the fireplace. When we did the room out it was found again. As a listed building we keep everything and put it in a display case. They might have taken it as a prank. Hopefully we will get it back."

According to local legend the ghost of the "Demented Whist Player" is said to haunt the pub with many visitors noticing a cold sensation in certain parts of the building. Staff also complain that items are moved or hidden but reappear weeks later.

This is not the first time the severed hand has gone missing. It vanished in March 2004 but was mysteriously returned six weeks later.

The severed hand of a cheating gambler ▲

3 Minster Street

Built:	Late 15th century
Materials:	Timber frame wall
Original purpose:	Home
Key feature:	Ornate bargeboards

3 Minster Street was originally built as a timber framed house in the late 15th century. Being a three-storey building with such striking gable ends, it would have been an imposing building in its time. The owners of such buildings must have been extremely wealthy, considering the enormous cost of building timber framed houses, not only because of the timber, but also because very skilled craftsmen were required to select, cut, join and peg the buildings' many timber components. It wasn't really until about 1180 that proper carpentry arrived in England. Although there were basic timber structures before then, they were built by craftsmen referred to as timber-wrights — not carpenters. We can date timber buildings accurately using dendrochronology, a process which dates a tree by comparing its ring-pattern and to a stored chronology of other patterns. In England there is a stored master sequence going back to 5000 B.C.

This building hasn't always been a jeweller's and clockmaker's. Built in the 15th century, it provided a home for wealthy merchants. There was an enormous stone fireplace in the main hall to let visitors know just how wealthy the owners were. In 1611 the house was leased by Robert Holmes, who made the big mistake of subletting it to another Robert – Robert Jole, brewer and mayor of Salisbury. This was a man whom his fellow aldermen described as "beinge of a moste furious and fierye nature". While he was mayor he got so drunk that, as he staggered back home, he fell into a "filthy miry ditch that runneth through the Greyhound ... getting out with much adoe, ... he walked through the river" to his back door. In those days the streets and

William Carter set up his watchmaking business in this building in 1817. ▲

canals were open sewers, so it's best not to try to imagine the state of him. It's no wonder, then, that Mr. Holmes did not trust him; so much so that he made an inventory of every removable object in the house, including window panes and bolts on doors. Later tenants and owners were more respectable. From 1615 to 1688, the house was let to a shoemaker, Richard Mason, who split it in two in order to accommodate the Cooper family who were also shoemakers. The house was reunited when Samuel Fawconer purchased it in 1741. Now, this was an interesting family. Samuel Fawconer (nowadays we would probably say Faulkner) also owned the Haunch of Venison next door and ran

an inn called the Lamb and Flag on the High Street. He and his wife, Ann, had two sons, Samuel and Edward, both of whom went to Merton College, Oxford. Samuel took Holy Orders and became rector of Poole and vicar of Osmington in Dorset. He was also a published author – *Discourse on Modern Luxury* (1765). His brother, Edward followed a very similar path, becoming rector of Upwey and vicar of Fleet in Dorset. The house remained in the family until James Fawconer, Edward's grandson, was forced to sell due to financial problems. Enter William Carter, a young watch and clockmaker who, in 1817 sets up shop on these premises. The business has been passed on from generation to generation ever since. The present shopfront dates from the time of a third generation William Carter in 1876. In 1911 Percy Holmes formed a partnership with the Carter family and today his great-grandchildren run the business with the charm and elegance of an age gone by.

◀ **Mahogany showcase.**

16 - 20 Minster Street, New Sarum House

Built:	1902
Materials:	Red brick, ashlar and timber bay windows
Original purpose:	Commercial chambers
Key feature:	Ornate decoration

This ornate building has a wealth of architectural features carefully composed and constructed from a range of materials in the Jacobean Revival Style. The Jacobean style was in vogue between 1600 and 1690, extending across the reigns of James I and his son Charles I. The Jacobean style represented the English Renaissance period, marking the transition between the Elizabethan and the neoclassical styles. The composition of the Jacobean building was considered to be a much freer arrangement of elements and this is reflected here. The architect, Fred Bath, has fused features such as turrets, pedimented bay windows and chimney stacks from ashlar stone, brickwork, timber, render, lead and clay tiles. The building was constructed at the beginning of the twentieth century and its ornate detailing means it would have cost a pretty penny.

St. Leonard's Church designed by Fred Bath (below) for Lady Louisa Ashburton in honour of her daughter Mary Florence Baring.

Lord Sidney Herbert, 14th Earl of Pembroke and President of Salisbury Constitutional and Working Men's Unionist Association, which occupied New Sarum House as its headquarters in 1912.

(as in Barings Bank – the one that collapsed in 1995 due to the antics of Nick Leeson). Throughout her life she was interested in the arts and was friends with many of the artists and literati of her day.

Frederick – Fred – Bath was a local boy. Born and educated in Salisbury, he became a very prominent architect of his time. In 1902 he had two big projects on the go. One was this one (New Sarum House), the other was the Church of St. Leonard in a village called Sherfield English. Fred, by the way, also designed the new façade of the Hall of John Halle (see page 44). The church was commissioned by Lady Louisa Ashburton in memory of her only daughter, the Marchioness of Northampton, who had recently died in her early forties. Lady Ashburton was immensely rich, having, in her early thirties, become the widow of William Baring Bingham

Until 1884 only men with property were allowed to vote in the UK. Sidney Herbert, the 14th Earl of Pembroke could definitely vote. He owned over 60,000 acres of land in England and Ireland and he was MP for Wilton. In 1884 the law changed. Men who paid rent could also vote. That meant that a lot of working men could vote, but – would they vote Conservative? Well, the Earl of Pembroke

lost his Wilton Constituency in 1885. The Conservative Party realised that if it was to survive, it would have to include working men among its supporters. Thus was born the Salisbury Constitutional and Working Men's Unionist Association, presided over by . . . the Earl of Pembroke. By 1912 the Association had outgrown its offices in Castle Street and moved to the thoroughly modern New Sarum House. The Earl died suddenly while in Italy the following year.

NEW SARUM HOUSE

Market House

Built:	1858
Materials:	Brick & ashlar, iron & glass roof
Original purpose:	Corn exchange
Key feature:	Half-round arches

The Market House, later better known as the Corn Exchange, and now the city library, was described at the time of its construction in 1859 as being "in the form of an ancient Roman basilica". Well, not really. In fact, it is very utilitarian. Like so many similar constructions which appeared around the country at the time, the round arches reflect an architecture accommodating the needs of a burgeoning railway network. Trains entered through the back of the building to offload corn, cattle and cheese – right in the heart of the city's market. The structure, designed by railway engineer John Strapp, displays an ashlar stone façade. Its interior would have been very impressive, originally consisting of a cast iron frame with wrought iron first floor balconies, all under a big glass roof.

Obviously, the Market Place is the hub of Salisbury, not only in terms of its present activity, but also in terms of its history. From the day New Sarum (present day Salisbury) was granted a Charter in 1227 allowing a market and a fair, this square became its centre of activity. It was here that, in the Middle Ages, Salisbury gained prosperity from the wool trade. Travellers going from London to Exeter (then one of the most important cities in England), passed through Sarum Market. Travellers from Wilton (then the county seat) to Southampton passed through Sarum Market – and spent money here. It

SALISBURY CIVIC SOCIETY

Andrew B Middleton MRCS
1819 - 1879

Eradicated cholera in Salisbury by replacing open canals with drains and covered sewers as recommended by the Public Health Enquiry held in this building 1851

◄ *Blue plaque dedicated to Dr. Middleton at 7-9 High Street (see page 50).*

17th century writer and diarist, John Evelyn. ▶

was here that grain was bought and sold, pigs were slaughtered, children got lost, deals were done. This was a bustling, prosperous city! 400 years later the Black Death had hit several times and things were not so rosy. By then the wool trade had declined and the market was only of local importance. On his visit to Salisbury in July 1654 John Evelyn wrote in his diary, *"The market place, with most of the streets, are watered by a quick current and pure stream running through the middle of them, but are negligently kept, when with a small charge they might be purged and rendered infinitely agreeable ... but now the common buildings are despicable, and the streets dirty".* He's talking about the canals for which Salisbury was famous as the 'Venice of England' –, but they were no more than open sewers.

"Sweepings from butchers stalls, dung, guts and blood, Drowned puppies, stinking sprats, all drenched in mud, Dead cats and turnip-tops come tumbling down the flood."
- Jonathan Swift on open sewage

Two hundred years and a few cholera epidemics later, the canals were covered, despite years of opposition, and underground sewers were built at the relentless instigation of Dr. Andrew Bogle Middleton. And that's not all Dr. Middleton did for Salisbury. Although by the late 18th century things were improving, what really turned things around was the arrival of the railway. After many years of arguing, – frequently acrimoniously – it was finally resolved to build a 'market house'. After seven alternatives had been turned down by various factions, Market House was finally open in 1859, together with a rail link which lead directly from the mainline to the interior of Market House. The man in charge was, again, Dr. Middleton. At the opening ceremony and dinner he was toasted and asked to make a speech. It was a long and bitter speech, complaining about the difficulties of seeing the project through. The next day's newspaper commented: *"the lengthy document was heard with much impatience by the company".* That's gratitude for you.

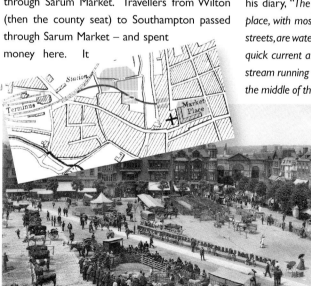

◄ **Map of 1885 with railway line running into Market House (modern layout in blue), and, below, 'Beast Market' in about 1903.**

Salisbury celebrated the coronation of King Edward VII in 1902 with a procession and then an enormous meal in Market Square. Note that there is a total absence of women at the tables! Men only. Women are on the other side of the hurdle fence looking in longingly.

GOD SAVE OUR KING & QUEEN

47 Blue Boar Row

Built:	About 1735
Materials:	Rendered brick
Original purpose:	Home
Key feature:	Quoins

This now seems a rather bland building. Some of its original features have been replaced: chunky glazing bars and nicely flawed glass by sliding plain-sashed windows; its brick and stone by render. However, its stone architrave surrounds, bracketed sills and arched head sections with a central keystone still survive.

The outside wall is render, divided by a raised band showing the intermediate floor level and a lead-covered cornice above the second floor, with a brick parapet on top. The roof's gutter is hidden behind this parapet so as not to spoil the appearance of the building.

The edges of the wall are detailed with raised quoins which give the building a certain sense of strength and presence.

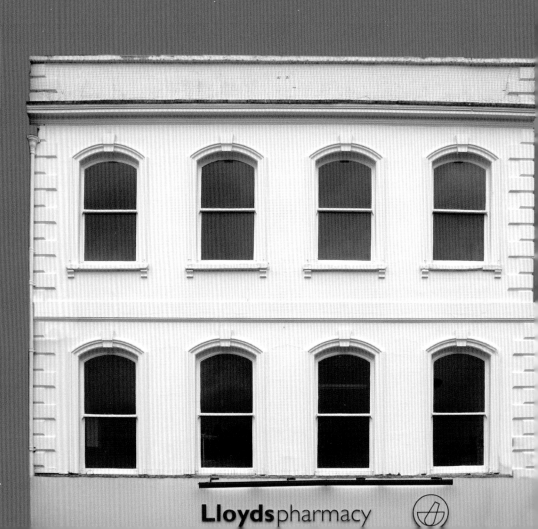

Lloyds pharmacy

Courtesy of Lion Television

"The Victorian Pharmacy" was an observational television documentary depicted by historian Ruth Goodman, Professor Nick Barber and PhD student Tom Quick on the BBC.

▲ **Holden's Directory of 1805 lists 47 Blue Boar Row as chemist's, 'Squarey and Pitts'. Note the arches in this early photo from 1838.**

Already in 1805 the ground floor of this building was a chemist's. So it has remained ever since. It was then called 'Squarey and Pitts, chemists and druggists'. Then in 1852 it became 'James Read & Co., Wholesale and Retail Druggists & Manure Manufacturers'. The 19th century was the heyday of the 'patent medicine'. A 'patent medicine' wasn't necessarily patented, in fact it didn't even necessarily have to work! All it meant was that the medicine was branded, usually with the name of the chemist who had dreamed up the concoction. By today's standards many medicines were not only ineffective, but plain dangerous. Lots of them included alcohol in their chemistry, but even worse, they contained ingredients such as laudanum and heroin. Nonetheless, some of these medicines actually did work. 'Baby soothers', such as Dalby's Carminative worked perhaps too well – they contained opium . . . one could say opium is quite soothing. The original Coca Cola was a medicinal 'pick-me-up' beverage invented by chemist, John Pemberton. The main ingredients were the coca leaf (cocaine) and the kola bean (caffeine). There were elixirs, such as Turlington's Balsam of Life (the bottles are very prized collectors' items nowadays). There were lotions, such as Elliman's Universal Embrocation, for aching joints and muscles, which came onto the market in 1847 and is still available today – and actually works! There were ointments, like Holloway's Ointment, which promised to cure old wounds, coughs, colds, sore throats,

Bottles of Turlington's Balsam of Life are a collectors' item today. ▶

bronchitis, liver malfunctions, and the "curse of sin". There were pills, like Hooper's Female Pills, of which Dr. Hooper said, "they are the best medicine ever discovered for young women afflicted with what is commonly called the irregularities and excellent for heart palpitations, giddiness, loathing of food, and likewise for scurvy". Toward the end of the Victorian era chemists were selling many patented medicines, but they were also manufacturing a lot themselves: aspirin tablets, photographic plates, condoms made of sheep's intestines or their own brands of perfume.

51 Blue Boar Row

Built:	14th century
Materials:	Timber frame, wattle and daub
Original purpose:	Home
Key feature:	Exposed timber frame

Until recently this building was tile hung with roof tiles on the first floor. The ground floor was rendered brick with a modern timber and aluminium framework. In the past, many timber framed buildings were given a brick skin, covering the wooden structure to make it look 'modern' – a product of fashion which ignored the building's history. The peak of timber-framing came between the 15th and 17th centuries, but gradually, as bricks became more available, timber-framing was seen as 'old fashioned' and shunned by the well-to-do. Behind many brick façades lay original Medieval timber framed houses. Nowadays, as in this case, exposing the original timber frame building with its wattle and daub infill is regarded as returning it to its original charming state. On the one hand, this process exposes the old oak structure to the vagaries of the weather, but on the other, it allows the wood to breathe. If wood can't breathe, it rots.

NUGGS 1268

Jotco de phugge

◀ **Johan le Nhugge, from his manuscript will.**

Many medieval street corners were named after prominent people who lived on the site. This is 'Nuggescorner'. The site was owned by Hugh Nugge in 1268. Very little is known about him, but we do have the will and testament of Johan le Nhugge from 1332. It refers to this house and, although not certain, it seems that Johan was Hugh's grandson – and a man of modest, but comfortable means. Judging from the six shops mentioned in his will, Johan was probably a tradesman. In fact, it's possible that his surname derives from the Latin, *nugigerolus,* a purveyor of 'fine clothing'. Like most people of his time, Johan was hoping for a pleasant afterlife. In his eyes, contributing to the Church was a step in that direction, so he left 12d. to the Cathedral and the same to the Church of St Edmund (now Salisbury Arts Centre), where he wanted to be buried. His wife, Edith, would inherit the family home and two adjoining shops; his daughter the other four shops.

Johan le Nhugge lived in interesting times. His life spanned the reigns of Plantagenet Kings Edward I, 'Longshanks', who sent the 9th Crusade on its way; Edward II, who was regarded as incompetent and was deposed by his wife, Isabela; and Edward III, who started the Hundred Years' War shortly after John had made his will. John knew about the capture of the king of France by the Black Prince at the Battle of Poitiers. However, what affected John most was not so much the victory of the Black Prince, but the calamity of the Black Death. During 1348 and 1349 about a third, perhaps a half, of Salisbury's population died from Bubonic Plague. John was lucky to survive and lived until 1359. Death on such a large scale left England with a huge shortage of labour, which resulted in great turmoil and culminated with the Peasants' Revolt of 1381.

▲ **The Black Death (or Bubonic Plague) of 1348-49 devastated Salisbury. It is calculated that the city lost between a third and half of its population. In this contemporaneous illustration, a priest is blessing monks already in advanced stages of the disease – note the pustules on their faces. Once contracted, the illness usually killed the victim within a week.**

◀ **The will of John le Nhugge from 1332. He survived the Black Death and died at a reasonably ripe old age in 1359.**

3 - 5 Winchester Street

Built:	About 1770
Materials:	Brick
Original purpose:	Hotel
Key feature:	Two architectural styles

This building clearly displays the scars of time. Although a single entity, at one time the building had two distinctly different architectural styles. On the left of the building, there are a series of very standard sliding sash windows over two storeys, but on the far right there is a pair of venetian arched windows. The shop below these venetian windows is in fact an infill of the original archway through which horses and carriages were taken to the courtyard behind. Given that the building is connected by the uniform treatment of the brick parapet at roof level, it seems that the venetian windows were selected as a means of 'marking' the entrance to the courtyard. There is another point of interest: the two sliding sash windows at first floor level on the right are set closer together than the pair on the left. Studying the brickwork immediately above these windows, it is obvious that originally there was a large projecting bay window here which has since been removed. The historic photograph *(right)* clearly shows this feature in position.

CAMBRIDGE WINE MERCHANTS

▲ **Horse racing in the 1880's.**

View of Winchester Street from Blue Boar Row in 1916. The bay window was still in place. ▼

Salisbury is divided into sectors called chequers – it's how the city was designed back in the 13th century. The Three Swans chequer was named after the inn that once stood here. The only part that remains of the inn is what was the warehouse over the entrance to the courtyard. Richard Figes inherited the Three Swans Hotel from his father in the 1870's. By 1882 he had gone bankrupt. Born in 1849 Richard seems to have been quite a fun-loving character. His passion was horse racing and gambling. He didn't just attend races, he was a professional starter – the man who drops the flag. Perhaps avoiding his many debts, Richard emigrated to Paris. A. Dick Luckman was in the 1880's a Paris-based sports journalist for the Daily Herald. In his book published in 1914 , *Sharps, Flats, Gamblers and Racehorses,* he writes: "Richard Figes was the starter at the majority of the meetings. Dick Figes came from Salisbury, where his father kept an hotel. He dispensed hospitality in his flat in the Avenue de la Grande Armee, and I ate my first Christmas dinner in France at his place. He was very fond of the best, which made his table all the more attractive. He was fond of practical jokes, and once he met a friend of his in the hall, saying he was just going to dress for dinner, as Lord and Lady So-and-so were coming. The poor chap who had been invited to dinner rushed off and donned his best 'soup and fish,' returning only to find Figes and I playing billiards in our shirt sleeves and no lord knows who!"

As a short, but poignant footnote, the trustee who administered the debt of Richard Figes was Frederick Aston Dawes *(see note top left).* His wife died giving birth to his only son; then that son was killed in the Great War in 1914, while his wife was pregnant with his first son – Fred's grandson.

◀ **Richard Figes, holding his starter's flag.**

39

13 - 15 Winchester Street

Built:	1926
Materials:	Stone
Original purpose:	Co-operative Store
Key feature:	Chequers of knapped flint

There is a Scottish Baronial quality to this building, which was designed and constructed at the end of the English Arts and Crafts period. The building is notable for its use of stone, combined with the composition of four strong gables and the symmetrically placed projecting bay windows, which give the building real presence in the street. In addition to the Bath Stone facing material, the gables display chequers of knapped flint carefully set out to fill the gable above the parapet line. Two of the original five rainwater hoppers and downpipes remain and the carved stone plaque clearly shows the date of 1926. The flintwork in this case is called 'flushwork', because the flint's face is laid flat with the adjacent stone. The flint will have been selected for its dark colour so as to contrast with the adjacent lighter stonework. The chequer pattern is more formally known as 'diapering'.

Robert Owen – Father of the Co-operative movement.

This building was constructed for the Salisbury Co-operative Society in 1926 – it says so on the carved stone plaque on one of the bays (*see top right*). Nowadays the Co-op is a booming industry covering banking, insurance, food, travel, clothing …funerals. It is owned by its members and profits are ploughed back into the business or used to finance charities. Food is purchased under the terms of 'fair trade' agreements. The bank does not invest in weapons or other unethical trade. Clothing is ethically sourced. Robert Owen (1771–1858) is considered the father of the co-operative movement. A Welshman who made his fortune in the cotton trade, Owen believed in providing a good environment for his workers with access to education for themselves and their children. These ideas were put into effect in the cotton mills of New Lanark, Scotland, where the first co-operative store was opened. Spurred on by its success, he formed "villages of co-operation", where workers would drag themselves out of poverty by growing their own food, making their own clothes and ultimately becoming self-governing.

Stone engraving, which stands for Salisbury Co-operative Society and the year of the building's completion, 1926. ▶

Plans for altering the building to add the carved panels onto the bay windows. ▶

Members of Salisbury Co-operative Society at a fête in 1913 and bus timetable advertising the Co-op from about 1930. ▶

Peter Daniels Archive

16 Milford Street

Built:	18th century
Materials:	Grey header brickwork
Original purpose:	Dwelling and workshop
Key feature:	Fire insurance plaque

Although the main entrance of the building is now on Milford Street, it used be on Brown Street, which is the elevation shown here. This building has a roof form, which is rather out of keeping with most Salisbury rooflines: it has been influenced by the Dutch gable tradition, where the roof slopes back in two planes, first very steeply from the eaves line and then again in a much shallower pitch back to the ridge. The symmetry of the roof is further reflected in the composition of the elevation below. The brickwork has been afforded additional detail by using blue-grey header bricks amongst the red ones. The blue-grey glaze on the ends of bricks is an effect achieved by applying salt while they are being fired in the kiln.

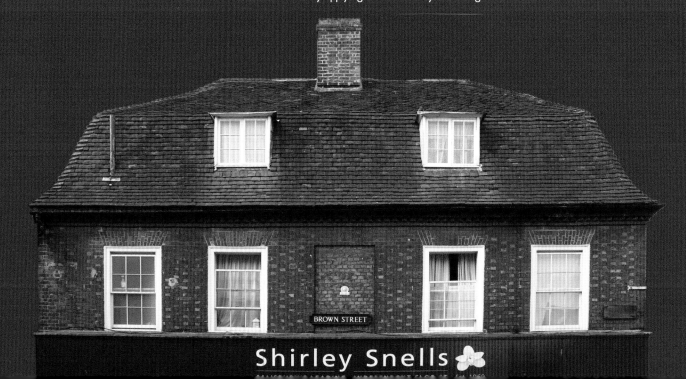

BROWN STREET

Shirley Snells

The destruction caused by the Great Fire of London in 1666 made fire prevention a must. Nicholas Barbon, a property developer, introduced the notion of fire insurance and formed the first fire brigade. It was cheaper to pay firefighters to put out the fire than it was to replace the building. The way it worked was that a 'fire insurance plaque' made of copper or lead, depicting the symbol of the insurance company was affixed to the outside wall of insured buildings. If there was a fire, the insurance companies would have a look to see if it was one of theirs. If it was, they put out the fire, if it wasn't … they didn't. Nowadays there are very few fire plaques still left in place, but there is one on this building. It's on the Brown Street side of the corner. The plaque has a policy number engraved: 380493. This policy belonged to William White, a tallow chandler. Yes, he made candles with animal fat. No wonder he wanted fire insurance. He also made soap by boiling tallow, which was a smelly business in a stuffy workshop. He would have undoubtedly wanted some fresh air. William lived and ran his business in Salisbury until 1786 when he apparently decided to move to London. The Salisbury

and Winchester Journal of 11 May 1786 records that: *"William White begs leave to return his sincere thanks to his friends and the public, for the very liberal favours he has received in the tallow chandlery and sope-boiling business …"* Then in 1787 the Humane Society publishes a statement to *"fully evince the utility of an air machine, invented by Mr. White"*, referring of course, to Mr. William White. His invention is regarded as important enough to be featured on the front page of The Times on 7 August 1789. The invention is a ventilator which would revolutionise coal mining safety by eliminating explosive gasses, and maritime health by providing clean air even when the hatches were closed.

Page from 'By His Majesty's royal letters patent. An air machine', by William White. ▶

◀ *After the Fire of London in 1666 new buildings were, instead of wood, made of stone or brick, such as the blue-grey header.*

◀ *Fire plaque is on the Brown Street side of the building. 380493 was the fire insurance policy number of William White, tallow chandler.*

8 New Canal

Built:	Mid 19th century
Materials:	Render over brick
Original purpose:	Printing Press
Key feature:	Large sash windows

There is an industrial charm about this rather unassuming building. Firstly, its windows appear almost over-sized in relation to the size of the building itself. Comparing this to a Victorian house of a similar period and size, there is a better balance between window and wall area. Notice also the distance between the head of the first floor windows and the sill level of the second floor: there is barely enough room to squeeze in the floor structure, which, given the use of the building, would have been designed to take the hefty load of cast-iron, steam-driven printing presses. Here we have a building designed for a purpose: to allow as much natural light as possible into each floor. In addition, the pairs of windows on each floor are very different from those on the other floors, which gives the building a lot of character. Most eye-catching is the raised lettering between windows, confirming that this building was indeed purpose-built as a printing works for a newspaper company.

As today, mid-nineteenth century politics depended very much on the media. Media tycoons had a great deal of power and Robert Farrant was one such tycoon.

One of the first provincial towns in England to have its own newspaper was Salisbury. William Collins founded the *Salisbury Journal and Weekly Advertiser in 1738. By 1780 it had* a circulation of about 4000 and still exists today, known as the *Salisbury Journal*. In 1808 William Bird Brodie, MP for Salisbury, purchased the *Journal* and made it the voice of the Whig Party for forty years. Whig policy was then mainly concerned with the supremacy of

parliament over monarch, free trade, expanded suffrage and the abolition of slavery . . . all of which the Tories opposed. However, the Tories didn't have a voice in the local press – until wealthy landowner, Robert Farrant, purchased the *Wiltshire County Mirror* in 1852 as an organ for the Tories *(see building opposite)*. At the time, North Wiltshire was represented in Parliament by Tory MP, Walter Long. Robert Farrant was concerned that Long would soon be retiring and his seat would fall into the hands of the Whig candidate, the Marquis of Lansdowne. Farrant reasoned that only Long's son, Richard, would be able to keep the seat Tory. He wrote to him to persuade him to take over from his father. Despite his father's opposition, Richard Long took the seat in 1865, with support of the *Mirror*. Walter Long died in 1867, but ironically, only one year after that, the much younger Richard Long also had to resign due to financial and health problems and died aged 49 in 1875. Nevertheless, the media was starting to show its clout.

Letter from Robert Farrant to Richard Penruddocke Long (pictured) encouraging him to stand as a Conservative for the North Wiltshire seat being left by his father, Walter.

Crime and Punishment

In 1847, Robert Farrant, who would later be the owner of the *Wiltshire County Mirror,* had a basket of apples stolen from his home. Henry Hall and Hezekiah and James Dear were found guilty of the crime, jailed for two weeks and privately whipped. The three were aged between 12 and 15. The photos featured here are genuine 'mug-shots' of imprisoned children from the mid-1800s.

◄ **In 1800 a printing press could produce 240 impressions an hour. In 1810 Friedrich Koenig invented the steam printing press, which by 1818 could produce 2400 per hour and, by 1848, the rotary press could print 8000 per hour – a revolution which made newspapers affordable to most people. This steam printing press is from 1860.**

15 New Canal

Built:	Late 15th century
Materials:	Timber and render
Original purpose:	House
Key feature:	Stained Glass

The Hall of John Halle is a building which displays centuries of evolution. Since its construction for the very wealthy wool merchant John Halle in about 1460, the building has had many alterations and additions, including two major restorations: the first in 1834 by A.W. Pugin; the other in 1880, by architect Frederick Bath *(see page 29)*, who designed the present Neo-Tudor façade. There are aspects of the building which are very special indeed, but let's focus on the stained glass panels of the original hall. These panels were installed by John Halle's son, William in the reign of Henry VII. They display heraldic roses, the Halle coat of arms and people such as Sir Thomas Hungerford, who was a friend of William. Stained glass is known to have existed in England since the 7th century. In Henry VII's day the glass colouring would probably have been produced by adding metallic salts. For example, sodium chromate produced yellow; potassium ferricyanide, red, and potassium permanganate, purple. The metallic salts were added to molten glass in a clay pot. The glass itself was made from a combination of sand, potash and lime and referred to as pot-metal glass. Stained glass flourished until the 1540's, but then the Reformation of the Church undermined the need for sacred artwork. However, it made a comeback in the 19th century when people like Pugin rediscovered medieval glazing techniques for the Gothic Revival. Frederick Bath also used stained glass panels on his extended front elevation *(see window on page opposite)*.

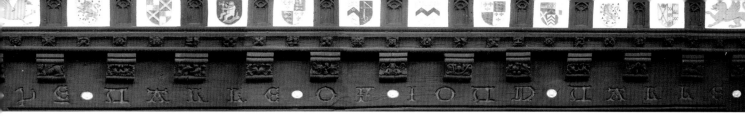

John Halle probably thought the earth was flat. When he died in 1479 Christopher Columbus had not yet discovered America. When he built this hall the Aztecs were still building their pyramids. He was a very wealthy and powerful wool merchant at a time when Salisbury was very prosperous because of the wool trade. He was so well off that to export his wares he had his own ship in Southampton. John Halle was mayor of Salisbury on four occasions and Member of Parliament four times between 1451 and 1465.

Perhaps he was too powerful, too rich and too stubborn. These traits brought him a lot of trouble. At the same time, there were a few powerful men in Salisbury. One of them was the bishop, Richard Beauchamp. In medieval times the people of Salisbury were practically vassals of the all-powerful bishop. The corporation of the city had certain rights under its charter, but the church owned most of the land. Another powerful man was John Halle's fellow merchant and bitter rival, William Swayne, who wrote to Halle stating immodestly that he was "as rich as thou, and greater beloved than thou"!* In 1464, while Halle was mayor, Swayne purchased a plot of land from Bishop Beauchamp with the purpose of constructing a house for his personal chantry priest. A 'chantry' was a fund, usually set up by the wealthy, to provide regular church masses for individuals. Swayne had a chantry altar dedicated to the Virgin for himself and his family at St. Thomas Church. Therefore, he needed a home for his priest – and land on which to build it. John Halle objected to this, claiming that the land was not the bishop's to sell. This became part of a dispute that had been raging between the corporation and the church for decades. Things escalated and in 1465 John Halle was summoned to appear before King Edward IV to put forward the case for the corporation. His representations before the king and the Privy Council only

King Edward IV sent John Halle to the Tower of London for sedition. ▲

earned him imprisonment in the Tower of London for sedition. The corporation were told to elect another mayor, someone "sad, sober and discreet", but the corporation refused because by then John Halle was regarded as a champion of the city against the bishop. Soon after, Halle was released under an amnesty and reinstated as mayor. The corporation did not allow him to appear before the king again, but he did continue to represent the corporation in negotiations with the bishop until 1478.

* T. J. Northy. "The popular history of Old & New Sarum"

68-72 New Canal

Built:	18th century
Materials:	Brick
Original purpose:	Warehouse
Key feature:	Cast iron cranes and overhanging roof

Some of this building's features are typical of warehouses from the late 18th century. At first glance there's nothing very notable about the windows, but look at the size of the windows in relation to the window panes: the windows are very big, while the panes are very small. That was intended to bring maximum light into the deep plan spaces on each floor. The same applies to the building at 8 New Canal *(see page 44)*, but this one was built at an earlier time, when glass was much more expensive. The small window panes indicate that they were very vulnerable to breakage and, of course, smaller panes of glass were cheaper to replace than the larger ones. However, the most striking feature is the combination of loading doors, cast iron lifting crane and overhanging roof section. All three worked in unison. The crane would lift the goods to each floor level where they were received by warehousemen through the loading doors. The overhang of the porch roof would protect the precious stock, keeping it dry and out of the rain.

At about the same time that the American War of Independence started, Francis Stokes set up his tea and coffee business. What has one got to do with the other? Well, tea was, to a great extent, responsible for starting the war. At that time tea was one of the pillars of the East India Company, upon which Britain was building its empire. In order to alleviate some of the economic ills that the company was suffering at the time, Parliament passed the Tea Act of 1773. This act exempted the company from paying duties on tea, which meant they could sell their tea much more cheaply and undercut their New England competitors who did have to pay the duties. This triggered a series of protests which culminated in the Boston Tea Party of 1773 – protesters disguised as Native Americans boarded a ship in Boston Harbour loaded with taxed tea and hurled the cargo into the sea. From this initial action came the slogan, "no taxation without representation" and from there the Declaration of Independence.

The East India Company may have been responsible for the American uprising, but, for Stokes Tea, revolts didn't seem important: while the French Revolution was still raging, Francis Stokes published this advert in the Salisbury and Winchester Journal:

Francis Stokes begs leave to return his sincere thanks to his Friends and the Public in general for the very liberal and flattering support he has experienced since his residence here; and especially acquaints them that he has laid in from the East India Company's last Sale an assortment of fresh and well flavoured Teas which he is determined to sell, free from any adulteration, at the lowest London prices.

Stoke's Teahouse at 53 Silver Street (now Boot's the Opticians) backed onto New Canal, next door to the warehouse. ▶

▲ **The Boston Tea Party of 1773 was the start of the American War of Independence. The British government taxed the tea consumed in its colonies, without its colonies being represented in Parliament. Hence, "no taxation without representation". Above left: The Coat of Arms of the East India Company.**

Peter Daniels Archive

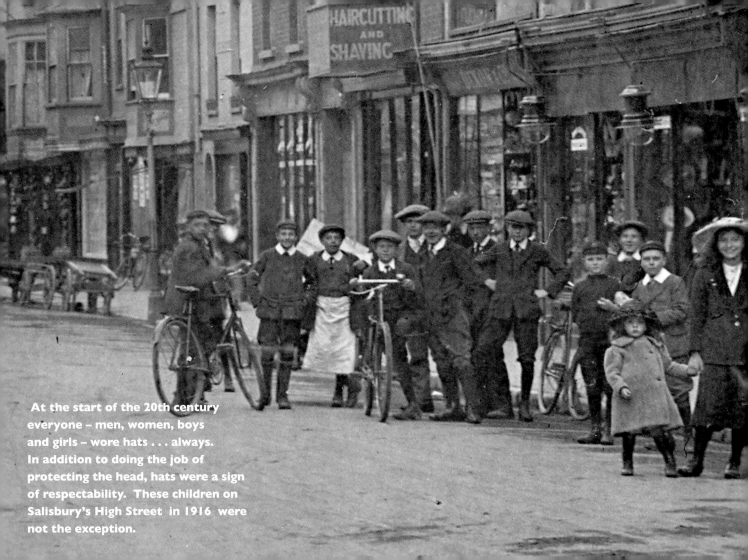

At the start of the 20th century everyone – men, women, boys and girls – wore hats . . . always. In addition to doing the job of protecting the head, hats were a sign of respectability. These children on Salisbury's High Street in 1916 were not the exception.

7 - 9 High Street

Built:	Early 19th century
Materials:	Render on brick
Original purpose:	Assembly rooms
Key feature:	Copper lantern

This elegant building, which sits on the corner of the High Street and New Canal is a good representation of the fusion of form and function. Essentially the long windows are designed to bring sufficient light into the first floor Danvers Room. Its elegance results from its use of the classical language of architecture and a reliance on symmetry. The building is thought to have been extended to its present form in 1802 and occupies the same site as earlier assembly rooms which were contained within the Fountain Tavern before it became the City Assembly Rooms and Literary Institute.

James Harris was a man of the Enlightenment: he was an admired philosopher, parliamentarian, grammarian, art and music critic, librettist ... and pretty good mates with Georg Friedrich Händel. For more than 50 years, Harris directed concerts and music festivals held in the Assembly Rooms – Händel's Messiah was performed here several times in the 1750's. Although these concerts were certainly held in Salisbury's 'Assembly Rooms', it is not clear whether they were held in these Assembly Rooms. This is the convoluted – some might say 'baroque' – story. A tavern called The Fountain stood on this site for many years. There was an assembly room attached to it where the cream of 18th century Salisbury society attended balls and gathered to listen to music. A chap by the name of William Naish published maps of Salisbury in 1716 and again in 1751. His

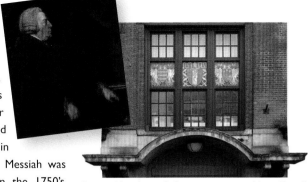

James Harris and the entrance on New Canal to Acland Hall. The other assembly room is the smaller Danvers Room overlooking the High Street.

▶ **In the mid to late 19th century, William Price Aylward, a piano teacher, took up the role from Harris organising subscription concerts. One major coup was getting Franz Liszt to give a recital. He had a shop on New Canal where he sold pianos and sheet music.**

◀ **Händel, reputed to have performed in Salisbury's Assembly Rooms.**

later map shows the 'old assembly house' on New Street (not New Canal!) and the 'new assembly rooms' at 57 New Canal (the side entrance to present-day Waterstone's – *pictured above*). However, and this is where the confusion lies, records show that this building was built in 1802. It appears that this is wrong, that the assembly rooms were already here. What might explain things is an article in the *Salisbury Journal* of 1 November 1802 inviting tenders to extend the building, "*adding two new rooms, with convenient offices upon the same floor, and a proper stair-case (with two entries to it from the street) to the present assembly room at Salisbury (which assembly room is intended to remain)* . . .". This explains the Blue Plaque on the New Canal side of the building. From about then, the festivals

that Harris had started became a triennial event, leading to the *Salisbury Journal* of 26 August 1804 to comment, "*there never was a more lovely display of elegant and beautiful women than graced each ball night at the Rooms, which presented a squeeze not to be surpassed at the splendid routes of the most fashionable in the British Empire*".

▶ **Clock of W.H. Smith – note that instead of numbers, the face has the letters 'WHSMITH&SONS'. The weather vane is a newspaper delivery boy.**

13 High Street

Built:	16th century
Materials:	Red clay hanging tiles
Original purpose:	Probably house
Key feature:	Ogee bay window

This is certainly one of Salisbury's more enigmatic medieval buildings and it carries a Listed Grade II* status. Most striking is its somewhat incongruous Dutch barn-like profile, otherwise known as a half-hipped roof. It is like this because at some time in the 18th century, the two gables of the original building were infilled to create further roof space. The unusual position of the high window confirms this. This strong roof form is counterpointed by the first floor angular bay window with its ogee lead clad roof, thought to date from the 16th or 17th century. An 'ogee' is formed by two 'S' shaped curves, which are a mirror image of each other and meet at the top, thus: ⌒. The ogee is commonly used in 14th and 15th century Gothic architecture one of the principal decorative forms. This ogee bay window has a continuous frieze and corner detail on which an ornamental diamond pattern has been incorporated.

The building is also striking because its whole elevation above ground floor is clad in clay tiles, which appear to cascade down its frontage. The 18th century casement windows are somewhat incongruous given that the original windows would more than likely have consisted of leaded lights similar to those found on 8, Queen Street (pages 8-9).

Frederick Sutton - confectioner and mayor of Salisbury.

Fred Sutton was larger than life. There is no official biography of the man, but judging from the scraps of information that have survived the century since he ran his restaurant and confectioners' here, it seems he was committed and involved in his community. In an age when class was all-important, he seems to have dealt as easily with his delivery boys as he did with army generals. His restaurant must have been fancy because he had a Swiss chef preparing food. He is mentioned twice in the 1897 book, *Popular History of Old and New Sarum* by T.J.

▲ *Sutton's Bakery football team in 1914 with Fred Sutton in centre. How many of the players would not return from the impending Great War?*

Northy. The first is regarding the chess club: *"the head-quarters were fixed at Mr. Fred Sutton's Restaurant where they remained till last year (1895), when, owing to an increase of business, a change of premises became necessary"*. Then he reappears as a conservationist. When doing renovation work

in 1893, he uncovered an Elizabethan oak beam with the inscription, *"Have God before thine eies, who searcheth hart and raines; and live according to his lawe, then glorye is thy gaines'"*. Northy points out that the beam *"had been covered over with paint by some person to whom such unique relics of past ages evidently had no interest"*. Fred Sutton also financed a local football team – Sutton FC (see ball in photo, left). In fact, he was so well regarded that he was made Mayor of Salisbury in 1913.

In 1913 the Mayor of Salisbury, Fred Sutton, held a banquet in honour of the 1st Wiltshire Regiment, returning from a two-year tour of duty in India and South Africa. ▶

Frederick Sutton's tobacconist, confectioners and restaurant in 1904. He is standing with the shop girls and delivery boys, the Swiss chef is 2nd from right. Also an invoice to "the executors of ◀ **the Late Mrs. Boyle".**

15-17 High Street, Old George Inn

Built:	1320
Materials:	Timber frame
Original purpose:	Inn
Key feature:	Projecting bays

Our high street buildings carry many stories behind their façades. None less so than the George Inn. Built in 1320, this presents a somewhat unfortunate case of extensive messing about: demolition, rebuild and attempts at restoration. Fortunately, and despite the number of amendments inflicted on it, this building was always seen as rather important. As a result, it has been well recorded in sketches and renderings — particularly in the 19th century and early 20th century. These sketches tell us much about the story of this building, including the fact that the windows on the third floor, above the projecting bays, had actually been covered during the 17th century and then reopened soon after 1900. Also, that the original medieval ground floor construction was largely swept away in 1967 to make way for a modern entrance into the shopping mall behind.

old george mall

Of the Old George Inn there remains hardly anything but the façade. Behind this façade there is a 1960's mall . . . and a long, rich history. In the hundreds of years it stood here, the inn witnessed great and terrible things. According to E.E. Dorling, author of *A History of Salisbury*, when the plague hit Salisbury in 1654, within five months 381 people died in St. Edmund parish alone. When the plague returned 15 years later, the memory of the previous episode was still fresh, so no one was visiting Salisbury, there was a "want of passengers and strangers". Robert Spikernel was landlord at the time, and times were desperate. So much so that *"he prayed to the mayor and commonalty, whose tenant he was, to forgive him half a year's rent".* This was agreed and though the plague raged on, the George Inn survived.

Many great and important people rested in the beds and ate at the tables of the George Inn. It is said that in 1608 William Shakespeare stayed here with his troupe of actors and rehearsed *As You Like It* in the gardens of the inn. Other guests included Oliver Cromwell and Charles Dickens, but Samuel Pepys seems to have been the only one to record his visit and give his opinion when he stayed here on the 10th of June 1668: *"Come to the George Inn, where lay in a silk bed, and very good diet, to supper then to bed. 11th. Up and down the town, and find it a very brave place. To Stonehenge . . . and so home to dinner, and that being done, paid the reckoning, which was so exorbitant . . . that I was mad, and resolve to trouble the mistress about it, and get something for the poor".* Oh well . . . you can't please everybody.

Samuel Pepys and the first page of his diary, dated 1660. ▼

Sketch of the Old George Inn in about 1900 by William Henry Charlton (Note there are no windows on the second floor). W.H. Charlton was born in 1846, the son of a prosperous grain merchant. When his father died in 1875, he took over the business, but retired by the time he was 36. With lots of money and time on his hands, he could pursue his passion in life – art. He is frequently described as a 'Victorian gentleman artist'. ▲

52 - 54 High Street

Built:	Circa 1341
Materials:	Timber frame
Original purpose:	Row of three houses
Key feature:	Gables

The detailed drawing of this building's timber frame *(see opposite page)* clearly shows the complexity and enormous amount of wood required for such a structure. All the timber junctions had numerous hand cut joints, similar, but on a larger scale, to the types of junctions used in joinery, including scarf and mortice and tenon joints. The joints would then be fixed together with timber pegs. Frames were normally of oak, although elm and sweet chestnut timber frames are known to have been used too. Timber frames over 400 years old are susceptible to all sorts of attacks. The two most obvious menaces are rot and insects. Rot can be dry rot or wet rot, but both need to be treated to avoid any loss of strength in the timber. The Deathwatch beetle can cause havoc in timber framed buildings. These creatures bore into the wood and lay their eggs there. They take up to six years to mature and take flight, but while they're larvae they munch their way through the centre of timbers until they are virtually hollow. By then it's probably too late.

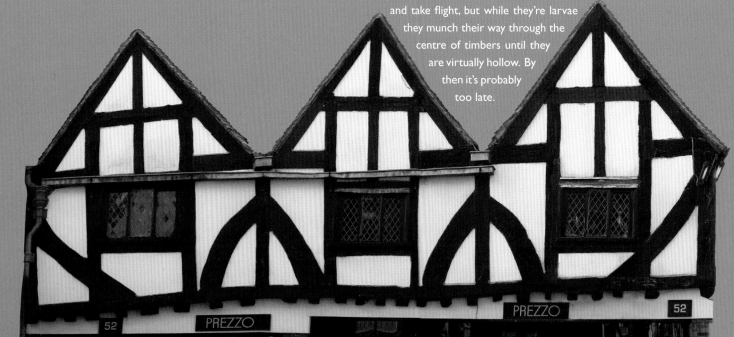

◀ *Browsing through the second-hand books just after VE Day in 1945.*

Timber-work, Hungerford coat of arms and King Edward III coin. ▶

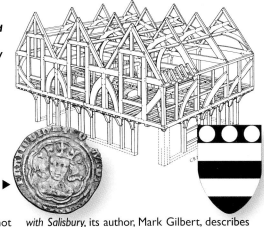

Beautiful and iconic, this building dates from at least 1341, when Walter de Upton, a very wealthy and powerful merchant, rented it to spicer, John of Shaftesbury. De Upton sold it to James Burgeys, who in turn gave it (yes, 'gave it') to Thomas de Hungerford in 1356, when Hungerford was High Sheriff of Wiltshire. The significance of this man is that he was the first to hold the title of 'Speaker of the House' in Parliament. It was rather bad timing on his part however, because he took up his post in 1377 at the beginning of Edward III's last Parliament – the 'Bad Parliament', when the 'Poll Tax' was enacted, triggering the Peasants' Revolt of 1381.

Then, in so far as this house is concerned, not much happens for almost 600 years,* until in 1934 Mr. and Mrs. Beach set up Beach's Book Shop. Beach's was the kind of bookshop with the rather musty smell that second-hand bookshops should have. A place where one could linger and browse for hours, until a book was chosen. In a tiny tome from about 1950 entitled *Some Early Literary Associations* with Salisbury, its author, Mark Gilbert, describes the owners: *"The genial Mr. Beach, and the very pleasant Mrs. Beach, are likeable people without any trace of highbrow nonsense. Beach is obviously a man's man, and a country type at that; and Mrs. Beach has a quiet half-smile all the time that makes me feel that she must regard work as pleasure. He does the buying; she does the selling and, incidentally, sees that the junior staff keep the books sorted, classified, and displayed. No grimy, dusty tomes will be found here!"*

* *Apologies to the many people who began, lived and ended their life under this roof, but very little is known about them today.*

◀ *Tomb of Thomas de Hungerford, the first Speaker of the House and his wife, Joan Hussey.*

51 High Street

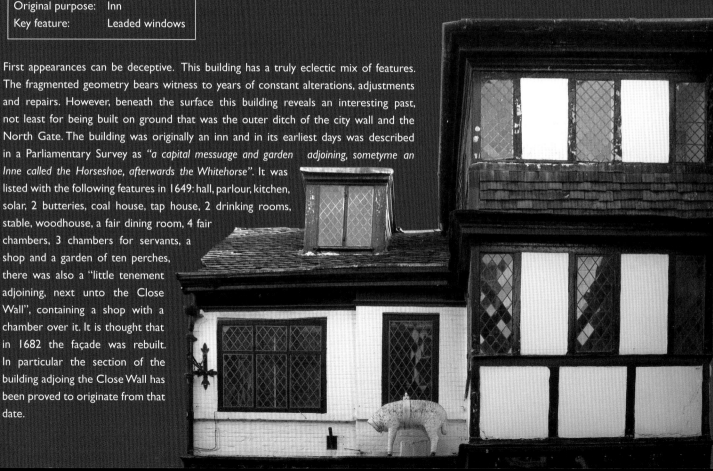

Built:	1602
Materials:	Timber frame
Original purpose:	Inn
Key feature:	Leaded windows

First appearances can be deceptive. This building has a truly eclectic mix of features. The fragmented geometry bears witness to years of constant alterations, adjustments and repairs. However, beneath the surface this building reveals an interesting past, not least for being built on ground that was the outer ditch of the city wall and the North Gate. The building was originally an inn and in its earliest days was described in a Parliamentary Survey as *"a capital messuage and garden adjoining, sometyme an Inne called the Horseshoe, afterwards the Whitehorse"*. It was listed with the following features in 1649: hall, parlour, kitchen, solar, 2 butteries, coal house, tap house, 2 drinking rooms, stable, woodhouse, a fair dining room, 4 fair chambers, 3 chambers for servants, a shop and a garden of ten perches, there was also a "little tenement adjoining, next unto the Close Wall", containing a shop with a chamber over it. It is thought that in 1682 the façade was rebuilt. In particular the section of the building adjoining the Close Wall has been proved to originate from that date.

Having lost a fortune gold mining in California during the Gold Rush, Joseph Lovibond returned to Britain to help his father run his brewery. He had noticed that the colour of beer was a good indicator of its quality and embarked on developing a system where colour could be objectively categorised. He failed with several systems, but one day in Salisbury Cathedral, inspired by the stained glass windows, it occurred to him that the answer was precisely stained glass. On that basis he developed a colorimeter called the Tintometer which to this day is used not only in brewing, but in myriad applications including dyeing, making steel, oil industry and water analysis. That's not the end of the story, however. Joseph had a daughter named Catherine, who, like her father, got things done. She had trained as a fabric designer and exhibited at the Albert Hall in 1900 with such success that she formed her own company, Stonehenge Woollen Industries. In an effort to create work in rural areas, she taught local women from around Salisbury and Amesbury how to spin, weave and knit. Later, after the Great War, she would also teach ex-servicemen and disabled people. When her father died in 1918, she set up a retail shop at number 51 and placed a wood-carved ram over the doorway. The shop remained there until 1959, when it was sold as a book shop, but the ram has remained . . . albeit headless in recent years. At the time of printing this book, the Salisbury Civic Society is in the process of returning the restored sheep to its place.

King James II had a nose-bleed which he saw as a bad omen and may have cost him his throne. ▶

Joseph Lovibond, a Salisbury brewer, invented the Tintometer, which measures colour to determine the ◀ *quality of beers.*

In November of 1688 the *Glorious Revolution* had just begun – James II versus his son in law, William of Orange. The first skirmishes had taken place in Somerset and the king had withdrawn to take refuge in Salisbury. He was staying in the Close when he was overcome by a severe nose-bleed. Dr. John Ballard was summoned and he rushed from his surgery at no 51 High Street to tend to the royal bleeding nose. King James took his nose bleed as an evil omen and decided to withdraw his troops, giving William a big advantage and, eventually, the throne of England. Dr. Ballard played a small but perhaps decisive role in the history of England.

Sheep before ◀ *it lost its head.*

North Gate

Built:	Circa. 1327
Materials:	Stone and rubble
Original purpose:	Defensive wall
Key feature:	Statue of Edward VII

A stone archway like the North Gate's, depends on compression (a pushing-down load) and can't take tension (a pulling-apart load) without collapsing. It relies on its own weight to create downward, vertical force. The gate is constructed from walls which are faced with random rubble and dressed stone, and then backfilled with smaller stones to make the wall thick and strong. In medieval times, there was no such thing as hydraulic lifting or propping equipment. They had to use ingenuity. For example to build an arch, stonemasons had carpenters make formwork (known as 'centring') in the shape of the archway. The stonework was placed in the formwork and, once set, the formwork was removed. The weight of the stone above makes the two sides lean against each other, creating a supporting action by pushing the load through the walls of the arch and into the ground.

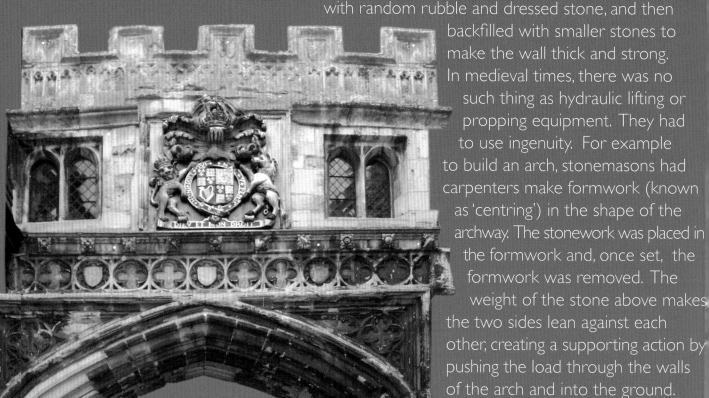

This is a tale of two Edwards – both kings of England – divided by 600 years. Edward III and Edward VII. In Medieval Europe, the king (or queen) had absolute power in the kingdom; even relatively minor decisions had to be made by the king or at least meet with his approval. For instance, Salisbury's boundary wall of the Close. It got royal approval to be built in 1327, the year in which 15-year-old Edward III took over the throne from his father, Edward II, who had rather made a mess of things and was forced to abdicate. Four years later permission from the king was sought to use the rubble from Old Sarum Cathedral for the wall. He approved. "You may use the rubble" are words he may have used – one can only speculate. Upon completion, there was a 13-foot wall and a ditch completely surrounding the close to protect the cathedral (today the west side is almost gone). Actually, to be precise, the initial permission to build the Close wall was not given by Edward III, but by his mother's consort, Roger Mortimer. Two years later, when Edward was 17, he led a coup against Mortimer and had him hanged, so by the time Salisbury requested permission to 'use the rubble', it was

▲ *Edward III came to the throne in 1327 when he was 15 years old and ruled for 50 years – he was a ruthless conqueror.*

Statue of Edward VII on the south elevation of the gate. It was placed there in 1909 to commemorate his visit to Salisbury that year. ▶

Edward who granted it. Edward III restored order to what had been chaos and turned England into a formidable military power. He began the Hundred Year's War when he declared himself the rightful heir to the French throne, gaining important victories at Crécy and Poitiers. He saw the country through the Black Death. He created a sense of national identity and chivalry – the Order of the Garter was his idea, for example. He was, in short, formidable.

On the south elevation of North Gate there is a niche wherein stands a statue. At first sight it seems to be the same age as the rest of the gate, but it is in fact only just over 100 years old, not 700. Perhaps because it faces south, it's had more than its fair share of wind and rain. It is a statue of Edward VII, which was placed there in 1909 on the occasion of his visit to Salisbury. He was in many respects, the opposite of Edward III. Unlike his predecessor, Edward VII was one of the oldest to step onto the throne and had one of the shortest reigns compared to Edward III, who had one of the longest (still one of only five British monarchs to have reigned for more than 50 years). While Edward III was ruthless and ambitious; Edward VII was socially affable, enjoying nothing more than hunting, gambling and womanising … allegedly.

Edward VII came to the throne in 1901 when he was 60 and ruled for 9 years – he was a leader of high society and fashion. ▲

Acknowledgements

For their support, encouragement and practical help, the authors wish to express their gratitude to:

Wiltshire and Swindon History Centre
Dorothy Treasure (Wiltshire Buildings Record)
Salisbury Museum

For their advice and assistance:
Louise Rendell (Architect at St Ann's Gate Architects LLP)
Richard Deane (Stonemason and Vice-chair of Salisbury Civic Society)

For their co-operation:
The Co-operative Society
The staff of Pritchett, Salisbury's finest butchers
The staff of the Odeon Cinema at the Hall of John Halle
The Tintometer Limited

For their excellent sources of information:
T. J. Northy (author of *Popular History of Old and New Sarum*)
Elizabeth Crittal (editor of *A History of the County of Wiltshire*)

For the use of photos:
Brendan McGhee
Peter Daniels Archive
Lion Television

About the Authors

Christopher Newberry is a freelance writer, designer and photographer who has worked as a producer and director of television documentaries and educational radio.

Rodney Graham is a practising architect and one of the founding directors of Design Engine Architects. He was born and has lived in Winchester most of his life

Christopher and Rodney have combined their interests and skills to produce an original visual perspective focusing on the relation between architecture, social history and high street environments to create the ***Look Up!*** series.

Also by the same authors:
Look Up! Winchester
Look Up! Salisbury
Look Up! Oxford *(to be published in July 2013)*

Look Up! Publications
www.lookuppublications.co.uk